This icon denotes a musical interlude
on the accompanying CD.

www.kindermusik.com

Published in 2006 by Kindermusik International, Inc.

Library of Congress Cataloging-in-Publication Data available upon request

ISBN 1-58987-164-2

Do-Re-Me & You! is a trademark of Kindermusik International, Inc.

Printed in China
First Printing, March 2006

Once Upon a Tune

Goldilocks
and the Three Bears
&
The Three Little Pigs

Two Musical Adventures

Adapted by Charnan Simon • Illustrated by R.W. Alley

Goldilocks and the Three Bears

A Musical Tale

Cast of Characters

Goldilocks
A curious little girl,
who is sometimes too curious for her own good

Papa Bear
A great huge growly bear,
who is much friendlier than he looks

Mama Bear
A medium-sized furry bear,
who is very warm and cozy

Baby Bear
A teeny wee fuzzy bear,
who doesn't mind sharing SOME of his things!

Once upon a time, there was a little girl named Goldilocks. One bright morning Goldilocks went for a walk in the forest. She came to a funny little house and knocked on the door. When no one answered, Goldilocks walked right in!

Goldilocks didn't know that this was the house of the Three Bears. Papa Bear, Mama Bear, and Baby Bear had gone for a walk while their breakfast porridge cooled.

It's a beautiful morning in the forest.

3

Goldilocks saw the porridge cooling. It smelled so delicious, she just had to try some.

First she took a taste from the great huge bowl. "This porridge is too hot!" she exclaimed.

Then she tried a spoonful from the medium-sized bowl. "This porridge is too cold!"

Finally she tasted a bit from the teeny wee bowl. "This porridge is just right!" she said happily, and she ate it all up.

 This porridge is just right!

Goldilocks felt nice and full. She saw three chairs and decided to have a little rest.

She sat down in the great huge chair. "This chair is too hard," she said.

She sat down in the medium-sized chair. "This chair is too soft."

She sat down in the teeny wee chair. "This chair is just right!" But no sooner had Goldilocks gotten settled than the chair broke all to pieces beneath her.

🎵📖 *This little chair's just right!*

Now Goldilocks was feeling sleepy. She went upstairs in the funny little house and found three beds.

Goldilocks lay down in the great huge bed. "This bed is too high!" she said.

She lay down in the medium-sized bed. "This bed is too low!"

Then she lay down in the teeny wee bed. "Ahhh!" she said. "This bed is just right!" And she fell sound asleep.

🎵📖 *This little bed's just right!*

While Goldilocks was having her nap, the Three Bears came home.

"Someone's been eating my porridge!" said Papa Bear.

"Someone's been eating my porridge!" said Mama Bear.

"Someone's been eating MY porridge," said Baby Bear. "And she's eaten it all up!"

"Someone's been sitting in my chair!" said Papa Bear.

"Someone's been sitting in my chair!" said Mama Bear.

"Someone's been sitting in MY chair," said Baby Bear. "And she's broken it all to pieces!"

"Someone's been sleeping in my bed!"
said Papa Bear.
"Someone's been sleeping in my bed!"
said Mama Bear.
"Someone's been sleeping in MY bed,"
said Baby Bear. "And here she is right now!"

 *We gotta find out who!*

Goldilocks woke up to find the Three Bears gathered around her. At first she wanted to jump out of bed and run away as fast as she could! But Baby Bear took her hand, and Mama Bear patted her shoulder, and Papa Bear told her not to be afraid.

So Goldilocks apologized for coming into the bears' house without first being invited. She helped Papa Bear make more porridge. She helped Mama Bear fix the broken chair. She helped Baby Bear tidy up all the beds.

Then Goldilocks and the Three Bears had a nice little party right there in the funny little house.

 Hi diddly dee dum, hi diddly dee!

The Three Little Pigs

A Musical Tale

Cast of Characters

Old Mother Sow
A kindly mother pig

First Little Pig
A light-hearted, carefree pig

Second Little Pig
A more serious and thoughtful pig

Third Little Pig
The cleverest pig of all

Big Bad Wolf
He huffs and he puffs, but he's mostly hot air

Old Mother Wolf
A kindly mother wolf

Once upon a time, there was an old mother sow who had three little pigs. "My dears," the sow said one day, "you are growing big, and the time has come for you to build your own houses. Now give me a kiss—and remember! Whatever you do, watch out for the Big Bad Wolf!"

"We will, Mother!" they promised, and off they went into the world.

 *Off we go into the world!*

The first little pig decided to build himself a house of straw. "Straw makes a cozy home!" he said.

The second little pig built himself a house of twigs. "Twigs are better than straw!" he said.

The third little pig decided to build himself a house of bricks. "Bricks are the strongest and the safest of all!"

 *A house just right for me!*

One day the Big Bad Wolf came across the first little pig's house. "Little pig, little pig, let me come in!" he called.

The first little pig remembered his mother's warning. "No, no, not by the hair on my chinny, chin chin!"

This made the wolf angry. "Then I'll huff and I'll puff and I'll blow your house down!"

And he did! Just in time, the first little pig slipped out of the back door and ran to the house of the second little pig.

 I'm a-gonna blow your house down!

The next day, the Big Bad Wolf came across the second little pig's house. "Little pig, little pig, let me come in!" he called.

But the second little pig remembered his mother's warning, too. "No, no, not by the hair on my chinny, chin chin!"

This made the wolf even angrier. "Then I'll huff and I'll puff and I'll blow your house down!"

And he did! Just in time, the two little pigs slipped out the back door and ran to the house of the third little pig.

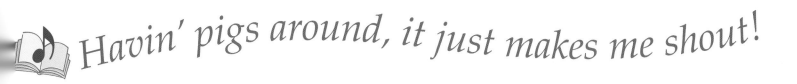

Havin' pigs around, it just makes me shout!

The following day, the Big Bad Wolf came across the third little pig's house. "Little pig, little pig, let me come in!"

But of course the third little pig remembered his mother's warning. "No, no, not by the hair on my chinny, chin chin!"

By now the wolf was so angry, he could hardly speak. "Then I'll huff and I'll puff and I'll blow your house down!"

But try as he might, the wolf couldn't blow down the house made of bricks. It was just too strong.

I'm the Big Bad Wolf and I don't like little piggies around!

The Big Bad Wolf was so mad that he sat down in the middle of the road and howled. He howled so loudly that his mother came to see what was the matter. When the old mother wolf heard the whole story, she made the Big Bad Wolf apologize to the three little pigs and help them rebuild their houses.

Then the Big Bad Wolf and his mother and the three little pigs and their mother all got together for a tea party in the pretty little garden behind the big strong house.

You've got to jump up, fall down, roll over twice!